African Celebrities

The Rise
The Legacy
The Future

By

Richard Owoeye, FCCA

Contents:

Foreword

In Africa's evolving social and cultural landscape, celebrities wield immense influence. This book by Richard Owoeye, FCCA, provides an inspiring and thought-provoking examination of how fame should translate into responsibility, service, and humanitarian leadership. It challenges the modern notion of celebrity and redefines success as the ability to uplift others.

Preface

The inspiration for this book arose from a desire to change the meaning of fame in Africa. Too often, celebrity status is associated primarily with luxury and personal recognition. Yet in a continent abundant in diversity and potential, fame can serve as a platform for advocacy, service, and nation-building. This book seeks to encourage those with influence to leverage it for the benefit of others.

In times past, people who impacted their communities positively were known to be celebrities as they were looked up to as role models. Today, the perception of fame has become increasingly complex and social media personalities can gain celebrity status almost overnight through content creation. This raises an important question—is this recognition driven by financial motives, or by a genuine desire to make a meaningful difference? Such ambiguity has blurred the understanding of what it truly means to be a celebrity.

Over the years, I have felt a deep desire to share my perspective on what it truly means to be a celebrity and to challenge the conventional focus on fame, luxury, and glamour, and instead highlight legacy, advocacy, and service. To every celebrity quietly making a difference whose name may not appear in this book, I hope this book encourages you to keep amplifying your impact within your communities. And to the remarkable individuals whose stories are featured in this book, though I may not know you personally, please accept my heartfelt appreciation and deepest gratitude for the inspiration you continue to bring to Africa and the world.

Thank you for being a source of hope, compassion, and inspiration. Thank you for showing us that making an impact on human life doesn't require grand gestures, but it begins with a kind heart and a willingness to serve. Your example continues to inspire countless others to follow in your footsteps and to believe in the power of humanity. Because of you, the world is a little brighter, kinder, and full of love. You have proven that the greatest gift one can give to humanity is not money or power, but love and empathy. Your legacy will live on through every person you have touched and every life you've changed.

For those whose names were not mentioned in this book, please know that this in no way diminishes your efforts; instead, it reflects the belief that Africa expects even greater things from you and your communities still look to you for more inspiration and impact.

This book will be available globally in both print and digital formats, with the goal of inspiring and celebrating meaningful influence across the continent.

Chapter 1

Redefining Celebrity in the African Context

Celebrity is fundamentally a social construct, reflecting individuals who gain widespread recognition through talent, accomplishments, or consistent public exposure. Yet, distinguishing between a celebrity, a public figure, and someone who is merely famous can be complex. While all three share visibility, celebrities often evoke emotional engagement and media fascination.

Historically, the concept of celebrity dates to ancient times, when figures like **Cleopatra** and **Alexander the Great** captivated societies through power, charisma, and legend. These early icons were revered far beyond their immediate realms. In the modern era, the rise of mass media, radio, television, and eventually the internet transformed celebrity culture. Fame became more accessible, and the boundary between public and private life began to dissolve. Today, social media further blurs these lines, allowing individuals to cultivate celebrity status through digital platforms, often independent of traditional achievements. Thus, celebrities continue to evolve, shaped by technology, culture, and collective attention.

In Africa, fame has never simply been about the spotlight. Long before flashing cameras and social media followers, African societies celebrated a different kind of star: the warrior who defended his people, the healer who restored hope, the leader who carried the dreams of the tribe. These were the original celebrities. They were men and women whose worth was measured not by wealth, but by the impact they had on their communities.

Today, the stage has changed, but the essence of fame should not. The African celebrity carries a mantle older than modern fame itself: the duty to inspire, to uplift, and to serve. To be a celebrity in Africa surpasses admiration; it is to be a **custodian of hope** and a **vessel of positive change**. Yet, somewhere along the way, the meaning of celebrity began to drift. Many of our youths, dazzled by the allure of luxury and popularity, have begun to equate success with material display. The danger lies not in the desire to succeed, but in losing sight of the values that once defined greatness—**integrity, hard work, and service**.

It is time for a redefinition not only of celebrityhood but of role models. True icons are not those who simply accumulate followers, but those who use their influence to build, to educate, and to heal. Across the continent, a new generation of purpose-driven celebrities is already leading this transformation. **Martins Vincent Otse**, widely known as *VeryDarkMan*, stands as an outspoken advocate for justice and accountability reminding us that fame should serve truth, not vanity.

These are the new custodians of African celebrityhood. The proof that influence, when wielded with compassion, becomes a force for unity and progress. But the responsibility does not rest on celebrities alone. Fans, too, must play their part by supporting purpose-driven initiatives, demanding authenticity, and celebrating compassion over extravagance. Fans can reshape what it means to be famous in Africa, because when fame serves the people, it becomes something sacred again—not just a reflection of success, but a beacon of hope for generations to come.

For example, to be a celebrity in Africa has meant being like the stars from faraway lands who have shiny cars, designer clothes, and millions of followers who adore them from behind their screens. Fame was imported, packaged, and polished. The more "Western" you appeared, the brighter you seemed to shine. But somewhere across the continent, a quiet revolution began.

It started with people who didn't fit the old mould: musicians who sang in their mother tongues, activists who planted trees instead of chasing cameras, comedians who turned pain into laughter like **AY comedian**, **Mr macaroni**, **Broda Shaggi**, **Basketmouth**, **Ali Baba** and fashion icons who wore their culture like a crown (**Lisa Folawiyo**). They weren't chasing fame; they were chasing *meaning*.

Take **Wangari Maathai**, for example. She never strutted down red carpets, yet she became a household name for planting hope, one tree at a time. Or **Temilade Openiyi 'Tems'**, whose raw, soulful voice carried the pride of Lagos to the world stage. Her fame wasn't built on glitter but on truth.

Across the continent, young Africans began to see themselves in these new kinds of stars. The boy in Nairobi realised he didn't need to sound American to make great music. The girl in Accra learned that beauty could be wrapped in Kente, braids, and confidence. The idea of celebrity began to shift from looking famous to *being impactful*.

Now, to be a celebrity in Africa is to be a storyteller, a changemaker, a bridge between the past and the future. It's about standing tall in your own identity, using your voice for something bigger than applause.

Think of the late **Fela Anikulapo Kuti** not just a musician, but a voice of rebellion. He sang truth to power when others were silent, turning his stage into a weapon of freedom. Or **Genevieve Nnaji**, whose calm grace and undeniable talent helped redefine Nollywood, showing young girls that strength and elegance can share the same skin.

Michael Collins Ajereh (Don Jazzy), who prefers quiet acts of generosity, changing lives without fanfare. Then there's **Damini Ebunoluwa Ogulu 'Burna Boy'**, whose global rise never erased his roots. He carries Port Harcourt in his rhythm, Lagos in his confidence, and Africa in his sound. His fame isn't just about charts; it's about changing narratives.

But not all is lost. Across West Africa, new voices are rising celebrities who use their platforms with purpose. People like **Angélique Kidjo**, who sings of identity and strength; **Davido**, who gives back to communities; and **Folarin Falana 'Falz'**, who uses music to speak truth to power. They remind us that influence is a gift, and it must be handled with responsibility, because in the end, the true measure of celebrity is not how many people watch you, but how many people grow because of you.

Chapter 2

The Anatomy of a Celebrity

What makes someone truly iconic? Is it their talent, their charm, or their ability to stay relevant no matter the cultural climate? The anatomy of a celebrity is a fascinating blend of personality, strategy, and timing. It's not just about being famous but about staying famous, and more importantly, staying *interesting*. In this chapter, I explore the key traits and tactics that help individuals rise to stardom and maintain their place in the spotlight.

At the core of every enduring celebrity is charisma. It's that intangible spark, an energy that draws people in and makes them want more. Charisma isn't just about being attractive or talented; it's about presence. Think of stars like **Beyoncé**, **Tom Hanks**, or **Zendaya.** They command attention effortlessly, whether they're on stage or simply walking into a room.

But charisma alone isn't enough. **Relatability** is the secret ingredient that turns admiration into loyalty. Audiences want to feel connected to their idols. When celebrities share their struggles or everyday routines, they become more human and more beloved. Social media has amplified this dynamic, allowing stars to engage directly with fans, share behind the scenes moments, and build a sense of intimacy that traditional media couldn't do.

Controversy, oddly enough, can be a powerful tool in the celebrity playbook. Scandals, whether personal, professional, or political, often thrust celebrities into the spotlight. While some fall from grace, others use these moments to reinvent themselves. The public loves a redemption; stories of resilience and transformation captivate audiences. They offer drama, emotion, and a narrative that fans can follow and root for. In many cases, a well-managed scandal can even deepen a celebrity's appeal, showing vulnerability and growth. Of course, not all controversies are created equal. The key lies in how the celebrity responds. Silence, denial, or arrogance can backfire. But honesty, humility, and a clear path to redemption? That's the stuff of legends.

In today's celebrity landscape, fame is a business, and the celebrity is the brand. Successful stars understand this and craft their public personas with precision. From fashion lines to fragrance deals, podcasts to production companies, celebrities are turning their names into empires.

It's about consistency, values, and storytelling. **Richard Mofe-Damijo** and **Kunle Afolayan** aren't just actors, but they are symbol of hard work, positivity, and hustle. These celebrities have built identities that resonate with audiences and extend far beyond their original industries. Social media plays a crucial role here too. It allows celebrities to control their narrative, showcase their brand, and engage with fans on their own terms. The most iconic stars aren't just known but they're *trusted*, and that trust translates into influence.

The relationship between celebrities and the media is a delicate dance equal parts love and war. On one hand, media coverage fuels fame. Interviews, magazine covers, and viral headlines keep celebrities in the public eye. On the other hand, the press can be invasive, critical, and relentless.

They leak just enough to stay relevant, tease projects to build anticipation, and use controversy to spark conversation. Some even master the art of disappearing and retreating from the spotlight to create mystery and demand.

Publicists, managers, and PR teams are often the unseen architects behind these moves, and they manage crises and shape the celebrity's image with surgical precision. In the age of clickbait and cancel culture, media manipulation isn't just a skill but a survival strategy.

Being a celebrity today is more than just being talented or lucky. It's about understanding the mechanics of fame and mastering the art of staying visible, relevant, and adored. Charisma draws people in, relatability keeps them close, and strategic branding turns attention into longevity. Scandals may shake the foundation, but redemption can rebuild it stronger than ever.

The anatomy of a celebrity is complex, ever evolving, and deeply tied to the culture that surrounds it. But one thing is clear: true icons *don't just chase fame, they shape it.*

Chapter 3

The True Essence of Celebrity

A celebrity should be more than a face on a billboard or a name that trends on social media. True fame carries a deeper calling of the power to help, to uplift, and to inspire real change. Beyond applause and admiration, the greatest celebrities use their influence as a force for good.

In Africa, a quiet revolution is taking shape. More public figures are stepping beyond the spotlight to embrace a higher purpose rooted in compassion and community. They are realising that *celebrity is not just privilege; it is responsibility.*

For instance, **Omotola Jalade-Ekeinde** is a shining example of what it means to wear fame with purpose. Beyond her celebrated career, she has devoted herself to philanthropy, youth empowerment, and advocacy for education. Through her foundation and humanitarian work, Omotola reminds us that influence is most powerful when it serves others. She embodies the ideal that celebrity is not just about being seen, it is about seeing others and helping them rise. Across the continent and beyond, this truth is being echoed by other stars who are using their platforms to drive social good.

Other celebrities like **Rahama Sadau, Davido, Don Jazzy** and **2Baba** in Nigeria have become symbols of what it means to turn influence into impact. Through education, empowerment, and advocacy, they are setting a powerful standard for humanitarian celebrity culture across Africa. Their message is simple yet profound: fame means nothing if it doesn't serve humanity.

That is why the truest measure of celebrity is not found in material wealth or luxury, but in impact in mentorship, service, and humanity. The message is clear: *true* celebrityhood is not measured by how high you rise, but by how many you lift along the way.

In Africa, celebrity isn't just about flashing lights, designer brands, or trending hashtags. It's about presence the kind that stirs emotion, moves people, and echoes through the streets long after the music stops. From the bustling corners of Lagos to the quiet towns of Enugu, Nigerians have always known how to celebrate stars. But the true essence of celebrity here isn't found on red carpets but in impact, authenticity, and connection.

The true Africa celebrity isn't only found among the famous. It's the teacher who inspires a classroom full of dreams, the fashion designer who weaves tradition into modern beauty, or the tech innovator who's putting Africa on the global map. These are the quiet stars, the everyday celebrities who shape culture from the ground up.

To be a celebrity in Africa is to represent more than yourself. It's to carry your people's story, their laughter, their struggle, their hope wherever you go. It's to stay real in a world that rewards imitation.

In the end, the true essence of celebrity in Africa is not about being worshipped. It's about being remembered for what you gave, what you stood for, and how you made others believe that greatness can grow.

Our films are winning global stages. Our sports champions inspire millions. Our voices shape culture. But today, we gather for something far more powerful than entertainment. This book is about impact, responsibility, and legacy.

We live in a time when young Africans no longer look only to politicians for guidance, but musicians, actors, comedians, athletes, and digital creators. Influence is power.

And with power comes responsibility. Fame is not the destination, but fame is a vehicle, and impact is the destination.

We see a beautiful transformation of celebrities who are choosing purpose over ego, service over hype. For instance, **Akon** lighting villages, **Sadio Mané** building hospitals, schools, and homes, **Davido** funding orphanages and giving scholarships, **Angélique Kidjo** empowering girls across Africa, **Charlize Theron** supporting youth health and rights, **Trevor Noah** investing in education and literacy. These are not acts of charity, but they are acts of leadership. A true African star is not just a performer, but a builder, a teacher, a protector, a visionary.

Today, the world can see the difference between publicity stunts and true service, camera charity and community charity, one-day handouts and long-term empowerment. Celebrities should not give to be seen but give so others may rise. Real impact does not demand applause, but demands courage, consistency, and compassion.

Every time you speak to a celebrity, someone listens. Every time you post, someone follows. Every time you act, someone learns. So, what are celebrities teaching? Luxury without purpose? Or success with meaning?

The fans know that the awards the celebrities receive will gather dust, trophies fade, charts reset, and trends change. The social media applause will disappear but the child who goes to school because of you, the woman who gets healthcare because you cared, and the village that has light, water, and hope, the young artist who succeeds because you believed in them—*that is your legacy which will last forever.*

Chapter 4

The Rise of Digital Celebrities

Traditionally, becoming a celebrity meant landing a record deal, starring in a blockbuster, or gracing the cover of a glossy magazine, but now all it takes is a smartphone, a Wi-Fi connection, and a spark of creativity. The internet has radically democratised fame, giving rise to a new breed of stars digital celebrities and they are rewriting the rules of stardom. From viral dance challenges to livestreamed confessions, the digital stage is vast, fast-moving, and fiercely competitive. But unlike traditional fame, digital celebrity comes with its own unique set of dynamics, risks, and rewards.

TikTok has become the launchpad for countless digital careers. With its addictive scroll, bite-sized videos, and algorithm driven discovery, it's turned everyday people into global sensations overnight. The platform rewards creativity, authenticity, and timing making it possible for a fifteen-second clip to change someone's life.

Digital fame is more volatile because trends shift quickly, and yesterday's viral star can become today's forgotten name. To stay relevant, creators must constantly evolve, engage, and adapt to the platform's ever-changing pulse.

Digital celebrities live under a magnifying glass, where every post, comment, and collaboration is subject to intense scrutiny. Cancel culture where public backlash can lead to reputational damage or loss of opportunities has become a defining feature of online fame.

Unlike traditional celebrities who often have teams to manage crises, digital stars are frequently left to navigate controversies on their own. A single misstep, taken out of context or amplified by online outrage, can derail a career. And because the internet never forgets, past mistakes can resurface at any moment.

Today's audiences expect transparency, growth, and responsibility. Some creators have successfully weathered storms by owning their errors, apologising sincerely, and demonstrating change. Redemption is possible but it requires authenticity and humility.

In the digital world, fame is measured in numbers. Followers, likes, views, and shares. These metrics are the currency of online celebrity. They determine visibility, influence, and even income. Brands look at engagement rates before signing deals. Platforms prioritise content that performs well. And creators obsess over analytics to understand what works.

But this numbers game can be both empowering and exhausting. The pressure to grow, maintain relevance, and outperform competitors can lead to burnout, anxiety, and unhealthy comparisons. Many digital celebrities find themselves trapped in a cycle of content creation that prioritises virality over creativity. However, digital celebrities are not just entertainers, they're entrepreneurs, marketers, and community builders.

They create their personal brands, collaborate with other creators, launch products, and monetise their influence in diverse ways. From Patreon subscriptions to merchandise drops, they've turned attention into income. So, what sets digital celebrities apart is their direct connection with fans. They don't just perform but interact. They reply to comments, host Q&As, and share personal stories. This intimacy creates loyal followings and fosters a sense of belonging that traditional celebrities often lack.

However, this closeness also blurs boundaries. Fans may feel entitled to access every aspect of a creator's life, leading to unrealistic expectations and invasive behaviour. Maintaining privacy while staying relatable is a delicate balancing act. Fame is no longer reserved for the few but it's open to anyone bold enough to chase it. But staying in the spotlight? *That's where the real challenge begins.*

The rise of digital celebrities marks a seismic shift in how we define and experience fame. It's faster, more inclusive, and more interactive than ever before. But it's also more fragile, demanding, and unpredictable. *In this new era, success isn't just about talent but about strategy, resilience, and authenticity.* The stars of today are those who can navigate the highs and lows of digital visibility, build meaningful connections, and adapt to the ever-changing landscape of online culture.

Chapter 5

The Danger of Misguided Influence

Social media has magnified every facet of celebrity life to inspire and the indulgent alike. In this digital age, fame no longer lives behind red carpets; it unfolds in real time, one post, one story, one viral moment at a time. And while this power can be used to build bridges of hope, it can just as easily mislead those watching from afar.

When celebrities use their platforms to flaunt wealth without purpose, they unintentionally sell a dangerous illusion that success is defined by luxury, not legacy. For millions of young people scrolling through their screens, these images become lessons, shaping what they value and what they chase. Yet, the true leadership has never been about display; it has always been about service.

Celebrity influence, especially in Africa, is a double-edged sword. Our continent's youth are energetic, ambitious, and increasingly relying on online platforms to look up to entertainers, athletes, and influencers as their role models. Their choices, both online and offline, ripple through communities, subtly shaping mindsets and aspirations. In a world where visibility equals validation, every post becomes a message.

When materialism dominates the spotlight, the consequences are profound. The constant showcase of designer outfits, exotic vacations, and luxury cars sends a silent message: *this is what success looks like*. And so, a new generation begins to chase glamour rather than fame over fulfilment. Education and skill building start to feel slow, outdated, even unnecessary compared to the allure of instant popularity and quick money.

But real success and the kind that endures are never built on vanity. It is built on purpose, resilience, and contribution. Africa's rising stars must recognise that their influence is not just entertainment: it is education. Every tweet, every photo, every public act has the power to inspire or mislead. The question is: *what story are they telling the next generation?* True celebrity isn't about how brightly one shines but how much light one gives to others.

In Africa today, celebrities hold more power than ever before. Their words spark debates, their fashion choices set trends, and their lifestyles shape dreams. But behind the glow of fame lies a quiet the danger of misguided influence.

Once, celebrities were seen as cultural ambassadors' musicians, actors, and public figures who carried the spirit of their people to the world. But in the age of social media, the line between inspiration and illusion has blurred. Many young fans no longer see celebrities as role models to learn from, but as templates to copy.

Take a walk through Lagos, Accra, or Dakar, and you'll hear it: "I want to live like her." Or "I want his kind of life." Yet often, the life they chase is a performance filtered, edited, and sold as success. Some celebrities, desperate to stay relevant, promote harmful lifestyles: glorifying fast wealth, fake luxury, or shallow fame.

In a region where millions of young people are searching for direction, this kind of influence can be dangerous. It feeds comparison, fuels insecurity, and replaces ambition with imitation. The boy who once dreamed of building something now wants to "blow" overnight. The girl who wanted to learn a skill now feels worthless without expensive clothes or followers.

West Africa doesn't need more stars who shine only for themselves. It needs lights that guide others not into fantasy, but into a future that's real, hopeful, and grounded in truth, for instance let's look at fame with purpose and stories of impact using some examples of the celebrities below:

These individuals show that celebrity is not just about admiration, it is about action. They are living proof that influence, when paired with compassion, becomes transformation. Africa's youth don't just need entertainment, they need examples.

Chapter 6

The Celebrity as a Humanitarian Ambassador

In the heart of Africa, a quiet transformation is taking place, one where fame is no longer defined by luxury, but by legacy. A new generation of stars is proving that celebrity status can coexist with compassion, that success shines brightest when it illuminates others. The late **Chief (Mrs) Irene V. Willoughby** more than four decades ago in the heart of Ota, a woman of extraordinary compassion and vision, changed the course of countless lives. In a time when abandoned babies were often left to perish in silence, she opened her arms and her heart to them.

At the heart of this movement lies the ancient African philosophy of **Ubuntu** "I am because we are." It is a reminder that our humanity is intertwined, that success is hollow unless it uplifts the collective. For Africa's stars, Ubuntu is more than a word, it is a way of life. By prioritising empathy, community, and shared progress, they are proving that fame rooted in humanity, creating deeper, lasting impact. Their journeys remind us that true greatness is not about being above others but standing with them.

Shaping Global Perceptions of Africa

Across the world stage, African artists are reshaping narratives and redefining global perceptions of the continent. Icons such as **Shina Peters, King Sunny Ade, Bright Chimezie, Nico Mbarga, Flavour, Paul Okoye, B.O.C Madaki, Peter Okoye, Burna Boy, Umar M. Shareef ,Wizkid, Davido, Kizz Daniel, Olamide, Phyno, Tiwa Savage, Sola Sobowale, Peju Ogunmola, Lanre Hassan,**

Jide Kosoko, Zachee Ama Orji, Adebayo Salami, Ali Nuhu, Richard Mofe-Damijo, Femi Adebayo, Pete Edochie, Kanayo O. Kanayo, Bolanle Ninalowo, Uzor Arukwe, Ronke Ojo, Toyin Abraham, Olufunke Akindele, Fathia Williams, Mercy Aigbe, Iyabo Ojo, Taiwo Hassan, Jim Iyke, Olayinka Quadri, Uche Jombo, Kate Henshaw, Iretiola Doyle, Ini Edo, Joke Silva, Mercy Johnson-Okojie, Stella Damasus, Uche Montana, Nancy Isime, Chioma Akpotha, Kehinde Bankole, Deyemi Okanlawon, Kunle Remi, Ramsey Nouah, Wale Ojo, Daniel Etim-Effiong, Timini Egbuson, Odunlade Adekola and Lupita Nyong'o have taken African culture beyond borders through music and film. Their work celebrates the continent's diversity, beauty, and brilliance telling the world a new African story.

Voices for Justice and Change

Beyond the realm of entertainment, African thought leaders are using their platforms to challenge systems and amplify the continent's voice in spaces where it was once silenced. **Trevor Noah** and **Chimamanda Ngozi Adichie**, through comedy, literature, and public discourse, advocate for justice, equality, and education on a global scale.

Nigeria's history is rich with courageous individuals who have dedicated their lives to truth and justice. Figures such as **Omoyele Sowore, Femi Falana (SAN), Tunde Bakare, the late Ken Saro-Wiwa, Dele Farotimi, Deji Adeyanju**, and the late **Gani Fawehinmi** have stood firm in the face of oppression. Their unyielding commitment to social equity and national progress continues to inspire new generations to rise, speak, and act for what is right.

Fame as a Force for Good

Legends like **Didier Drogba** and **Wole Soyinka** embody the power of influence as a tool for peace, democracy, and reform, proving that celebrity can indeed serve as an instrument of unity and healing. Their advocacy underscores a profound truth: *fame finds its highest purpose in service.*

These icons demonstrate that personal success and social responsibility are not opposing pursuits but complementary paths. They remind us that true influence is not measured by how many people watch, but by how many lives are transformed. Africa's stars are not only entertaining the world they are enlightening it. Their fame is not merely celebrated; it is *felt.*

Stories of Purpose and Impact

Consider **Rufai Oseni**, the Nigerian journalist who turned personal success into community service. In his hometown, he established a library and development centre—not for recognition, but for the future. His initiative has trained over twenty teachers and partnered with the *One Million Teachers* platform to strengthen grassroots education. Rufai's story reminds us that impact does not require a stage, only a heart.

In Kenya, **Lupita Nyong'o** uses her global platform to advocate for girls' education and gender equality, inspiring young women to dream boldly and rise fearlessly. In Ghana, **Sarkodie** channels his influence into youth empowerment and health campaigns, mentoring the next generation and proving that success without service is hollow. Together, these icons illustrate that true leadership begins when fame becomes a force for others.

Beyond Charity: Building Sustainable Change

To create lasting impact, African and global influencers alike must move beyond one-time donations toward programmes that sustain communities long after the spotlight fades—much like the **Leonardo DiCaprio Foundation**, which funds long-term environmental projects with measurable outcomes. Collaboration also builds credibility: partnering with grassroots organisations, researchers, and policymakers ensures that every effort is both effective and informed.

Education and awareness remain powerful tools for transformation. Using platforms to inform and inspire can spark understanding and drive action just as **Oprah Winfrey's Book Club** turned reading into a catalyst for social consciousness on topics such as race, mental health, and justice.

In the digital era, social media has evolved beyond self-promotion into a force for mobilisation. Campaigns like **BTS**'s "Love Myself" partnership with UNICEF show how online engagement can raise millions and ignite global conversations about self-worth, compassion, and collective responsibility.

Redefining Influence

Africa's brightest stars are redefining what it means to be influential. They are proving that the truest use of fame is not to shine alone, but to *illuminate others*. In the end, what truly matters is not who was seen but who was helped. That is the kind of fame the world will never forget.

Chapter 7

Impacts of African Celebrities on Charities

This publication extends heartfelt appreciation to all African celebrities who have made significant contributions to human development and societal well-being. It honours those whose names appear throughout this book. The message contained herein, now circulated across the world, is one of gratitude and recognition for individuals whose lives and actions exemplify purpose, compassion, and service to humanity.

Few forces are more powerful than a life dedicated to purpose. The African celebrities celebrated in these pages embody this truth. Through their actions, words, and empathy, they have touched countless lives in profound and lasting ways. Their greatness is not defined by wealth, fame, or public acclaim, but by the enduring positive difference they make in the lives of others.

From the outset, this book highlights how these celebrities embody a rare combination of humility and strength. They demonstrate that even small acts of kindness can ripple outwards to inspire transformation within communities. Their unwavering belief in the potential of humanity allows them to see good where others see flaws, hope where others see despair, and possibility where others see limitation. Through their compassion and encouragement, they have helped many rediscover their worth and rebuild confidence in themselves.

The influence of these individuals extends far beyond personal encounters, and it strengthens communities and, ultimately, enriches humanity. In a world often shadowed by division, fear, and indifference, their lives stand as a testament to the enduring power of empathy and service. Their leadership is not rooted in authority or control but in their commitment to serve others.

Despite the challenges they have faced, these celebrities have shown resilience and grace. Rather than succumbing to hardship, they have transformed their experiences into sources of inspiration, guiding others through similar struggles. Their stories underscore the central theme of this work

Across Africa, numerous public figures are leveraging their platforms to drive social impact, expand educational access, and foster sustainable development. The following profiles highlight influential artists, actors, and athletes whose philanthropic work continues to transform communities across the continent.

Omotola Jalade-Ekeinde

Through her *OYEP Foundation*, Omotola Jalade-Ekeinde empowers young Africans by providing educational and entrepreneurial tools that promote independence and sustainable livelihoods.

Nwankwo Kanu

Former footballer Nwankwo Kanu established the *Kanu Heart Foundation* (KHF) following his own life-saving heart surgery in 1999. The foundation provides medical assistance to children and young adults with heart conditions across Africa, offering them access to treatment and renewed hope.

Mansura Isah

Renowned actress Mansura Isah turned her public influence into a force for good with the *Today Life Foundation*. What began as a modest effort to support the poor has grown into a national initiative offering food, clothing, and emotional support to orphans and vulnerable families. The foundation collaborates with philanthropists and donors to channel aid to those most in need.

Hadiza Aliyu Gabon

Admired for her talent and humility, Hadiza Gabon founded the *Hadiza Aliyu Gabon Foundation* (HAG Foundation) to champion education, healthcare, and food security. Through scholarships, medical outreach, and food distribution, the foundation embodies her belief that "every life matters" and continues to uplift marginalised Nigerians.

Tonto Dikeh

Through the *Tonto Dikeh Foundation*, the actress advocates for widows, survivors of abuse, and underprivileged children, emphasising that compassion is one of humanity's greatest strengths.

Tiwa Savage

Singer Tiwa Savage uses her platform to promote women's empowerment and child rights, inspiring young girls across Africa to embrace confidence, courage, and self-worth through her music and advocacy.

Innocent Ujah Idibia (2Baba)

2Baba channels his influence into civic education through the *Vote Not Fight* campaign, which promotes peace and youth participation in democratic processes. His work underscores the importance of integrity and ethical leadership.

Florence Ifeoluwa Otedola (DJ Cuppy)

As founder of the *Cuppy Foundation*, DJ Cuppy advances education, health, and social inclusion for disadvantaged communities across Nigeria. Her philanthropic mission reflects a deep commitment to giving every individual an equal chance to thrive.

David Adedeji Adeleke (Davido)

Internationally acclaimed artist Davido established the *David Adeleke Foundation (DAF)* to support orphanages and child welfare initiatives. His public fundraising campaigns totalling ₦250–₦300 million have funded scholarships, healthcare interventions, and relief for hundreds of orphanages nationwide.

Ayodeji Ibrahim Balogun (Wizkid)

Wizkid's philanthropic endeavours include scholarships and donations supporting education and healthcare. His celebrity status amplifies the visibility and reaches of local NGOs and community-based programmes.

Akon

Through *Akon Lighting Africa*, the artist and entrepreneur has expanded access to electricity across the continent by implementing solar-powered infrastructure. The initiative has created jobs, enabled health centres to operate sustainably, and improved the quality of life in numerous rural communities.

Sadio Mané

The Senegalese footballer has invested directly in infrastructure projects in his hometown of Bambali, funding the construction of a hospital and school. His contributions during the COVID-19 pandemic further strengthened national healthcare responses.

Didier Drogba

The *Didier Drogba Foundation* supports education, healthcare, and emergency response initiatives across Côte d'Ivoire. The foundation's work during the Ebola crisis and beyond has strengthened health systems and expanded access to education for disadvantaged youth.

Samuel Eto'o

Through the *Samuel Eto'o Foundation*, the football icon funds education and health programmes for vulnerable children and refugees. The foundation partners with international organisations, including the FIFA Foundation, to promote youth development and social inclusion through sport.

Mohamed Salah

Mohamed Salah has made significant contributions to Egypt's health sector, donating to hospitals, funding medical equipment, and supporting cancer and emergency care facilities. His philanthropy continues to enhance the country's healthcare infrastructure and charitable outreach.

Bonang Matheba

Media personality Bonang Matheba is a prominent advocate for education and women's economic empowerment. Her initiatives promote access to scholarships and professional development, embodying the principle that "empowerment begins when one woman lifts another".

Charlize Theron

The *Charlize Theron Africa Outreach Project* (CTAOP) focuses on youth sexual and reproductive health and rights, as well as gender-based violence prevention across Southern Africa. The organisation's grant-making and partnerships have strengthened grassroots NGOs and improved community health outcomes.

Funke Akindele's newly launched charity initiative in Lagos is dedicated to empowering underprivileged communities by providing access to education, healthcare, and skills development opportunities.

Yvonne Chaka Chaka

Through the *Princess of Africa Foundation*, singer Yvonne Chaka Chaka champions literacy, women's empowerment, and child protection. Her advocacy and fundraising efforts have supported organisations such as Save the Children and other African NGOs.

Angélique Kidjo

Co-founder of the *Batonga Foundation*, Angélique Kidjo empowers adolescent girls in Benin through education and leadership programmes. As a UNICEF Goodwill Ambassador, she continues to advocate globally for child rights and gender equality.

Lupita Nyong'o

The award-winning actress uses her platform to promote education, environmental conservation, and cultural awareness. Through partnerships with initiatives such as WildAid, she advocates for wildlife protection and youth empowerment, amplifying the reach of local charities and cultural projects.

Banky W is a co-founder of the I-AM-CAPABLE Charity Foundation, established alongside his friends Segun and Tunde Demuren. The foundation operates under the broader Empire Mates Entertainment (EME) brand. In addition to his work with I-AM-CAPABLE, Banky W has supported other philanthropic initiatives, including the "Haven Helping Hands" Foundation.

Rufai Oseni

The Oseni Centre, an initiative dedicated to empowering local communities through direct engagement and inspiring thousands of young people across Nigeria through virtual outreach.

Ojinika Anne Okpe

The Ojy Okpe Foundation is committed to supporting underprivileged children, particularly those battling illnesses such as HIV and cancer. The foundation also extends its care to homeless and abandoned children, offering them hope, support, and a chance at a better future.

Martins Vincent Otse

The VeryDarkMan Foundation is a registered non-profit civic organization committed to exposing corruption, upholding truth, and advocating for justice in Nigeria. The Foundation strives to empower citizens to speak out against injustice rather than remain silent.

Chapter 8
The Role Model for Future Generations

When a star rises in Africa, they do not rise alone; their journey becomes a map for others to follow. That is why every celebrity must recognise the silent classroom they lead. Their lives, both public and private, can either inspire greatness or glorify emptiness. True success, after all, is hollow when it does not uplift others.

True influence begins with compassion. When celebrities visit communities in need, speak out on mental health, or take a stand against injustice, they show that fame can have a human face. Empathy is *the foundation* of meaningful public engagement, especially in West Africa, where communities often place high value on respect, relationship building, and collective understanding.

In contemporary Nigeria, fame brings both influence and responsibility. Celebrities who connect authentically with their audiences earn lasting respect and trust. The following principles outline practical ways for public figures to deepen that connection:

1. Communicate with Understanding

Engaging audiences across Nigeria's diverse regions requires sensitivity to local languages and cultures. Employ interpreters where necessary and prioritise active listening. Reflecting what you've heard demonstrates empathy and builds trust.

2. Respect Local Values

Before launching campaigns or charitable initiatives, involve traditional leaders, women's groups, and youth representatives. Dress and behave appropriately within each cultural context. Simple gestures, such as a Yoruba greeting or a respectful bow, can open doors and convey profound respect.

3. Share Your Story

Personal narratives foster connection. Celebrities who openly share experiences of unemployment, rejection, or humble beginnings remind fans that success is attainable and humanise their public persona.

4. Collaborate, Don't Dictate

Community involvement from the outset strengthens projects. Respect every voice, including those of marginalised groups or persons with disabilities. Inclusion not only builds loyalty but also fosters meaningful engagement.

5. Show Compassion and Accountability

In times of crisis, acknowledge people's pain before presenting solutions. Words should be accompanied by concrete actions and promises must be honoured. Authentic empathy builds credibility and influence.

Humility as a Leadership Principle

Humility is evident in how leaders and celebrities treat others. **Thomas Sankara**, for example, walked among citizens and greeted everyone from drivers to journalists, demonstrating equality and approachability. Similarly, **Angélique Kidjo** champions African identity while using her platform to uplift others. True icons avoid ostentatious displays of wealth; as footballer **Sadio Mané** observed, simplicity often speaks louder than status.

Remaining teachable and accessible is also essential. Figures such as **Ngozi Okonjo-Iweala** and **Chimamanda Ngozi Adichie** exemplify lifelong learning, showing that humility strengthens leadership. In essence, humility is not weakness; it is refined strength that transforms celebrities into enduring African legends, such as **King Sunny Ade.**

Collective Responsibility and Social Impact
Across Africa, genuine success transcends personal wealth or fame it is measured by the ability to uplift others. Leaders

from **Nelson Mandela** to **Desmond Tutu** demonstrated that societal progress arises from collective strength. **Wangari Maathai**'s mobilisation of tree-planting initiatives in Kenya illustrates how action often speaks louder than words. Celebrities can similarly champion youth centres, environmental cleanups, or community initiatives. African traditions, such as Rwanda's *Umuganda* or West Africa's *Esusu*, exemplify communal responsibility and collective effort.

Ellen Johnson Sirleaf's empowerment of women in Liberia underscores the principle of service above self. Every public figure has the potential to inspire community engagement, turning fame into a force for unity and hope. African proverbs like "the child belongs to everyone" remind us that solidarity strengthens societies particularly during crises such as the Ebola outbreak. By supporting orphanages, elder care, and neighbourhood welfare, celebrities can model compassionate leadership. Systems like Botswana's *kgotla* and Nigeria's local watch groups further demonstrate how participation reinforces democratic values.

True influence is grounded in consistency: empathy, humility, and integrity both on and off stage. Africa's future relies not only on elected leaders but also on cultural role models. Fame is fleeting, but impact endures. The greatest stars are not those most followed, but those who lead with purpose, compassion, and a commitment to collective progress.

Chapter 9

The Economics of Influence

In today's Africa, fame is more than glitz and glamour, it is *currency*. The rise of African celebrities had reshaped the continent's cultural and economic landscape, turning influence into investment and visibility into value. From music stages to business boardrooms, these public figures are redefining what it means to lead, build, and give back.

Take **Burna Boy**, for instance. Every international tour he embarks on doesn't just sell out arenas, it breathes life into local economies, creating jobs for vendors, promoters, and small businesses. **Davido**, beyond his chart-topping hits, invests in education, healthcare, and disaster relief, proving that fame can fund compassion. **Banky W** uses his platform to mentor young artists and champion civic engagement, while **Tiwa Savage** blends her commercial ventures with advocacy for women's rights and empowerment. These stories echo a growing truth: *African celebrities are not just icons, they are catalysts for sustainable development.*

Imagine the impact of businesses that prioritise sustainability, inclusivity, and community development. Just as **Akon**'s Lighting Africa brought power to thousands of homes, African stars can replicate and redefine these models to fit their own contexts of transforming influence into impact.

Endorsements are powerful, but integrity is priceless. By choosing to collaborate with brands that reflect their personal and social values, public figures safeguard their credibility and deepen public trust. In an age where audiences demand authenticity, aligning with ethical partners ensures that every collaboration strengthens their brand integrity.

Philanthropy should go beyond occasional acts of charity. True corporate social responsibility (CSR) becomes meaningful when it's woven into one's personal and professional identity. Much like **Leonardo DiCaprio**'s Foundation, which influences both conservation and policy, African celebrities can leverage their platforms to drive systemic change, not just momentary relief.

Transparency builds trust by tracking, evaluating, and openly sharing the outcomes of their social initiatives. Leaders can demonstrate that their efforts produce real, measurable transformation not just headlines or photo opportunities. The era of performative activism is over. True impact comes from sustained effort and genuine commitment. When advocacy becomes a lifestyle rather than a trend, it evolves into legacy.

In Africa, where the divide between wealth and poverty remains profound, philanthropy must evolve beyond traditional charity to become a catalyst for transformative change. Across both urban centres and rural communities, the influence of public figures is considerable. Every performance, endorsement, or social media engagement carries the potential to inspire millions. However, genuine impact arises when generosity is intentional, structured, and sustainable. To ensure that giving is both meaningful and enduring, several strategic principles are essential.

First, every act of giving should be anchored in vision. Whether advancing access to education, healthcare, or environmental sustainability, philanthropic efforts achieve lasting impact when guided by clearly defined objectives that align with personal values and the specific needs of communities.

Second, sustainable change emerges from partnership rather than prescription. Engaging communities in the design and implementation of initiatives fosters ownership, accountability, and long-term success. Influence is further amplified when public figures mobilise audiences to become active allies raising awareness, sharing compelling narratives, and championing causes that matter.

Third, tracking progress and communicating authentic outcomes transform generosity into a model that others can emulate. The future of philanthropy rests on sustainability, exemplified by social enterprises such as Akon Lighting Africa, which demonstrate how purpose and profit can co-exist, generating growth without creating dependency.

Across the continent, philanthropists including **Aliko Dangote**, **Folorunsho Alakija**, **Tony Elumelu**, **Femi Otedola**, **Jim Ovia**, **Mike Adenuga**, **Abdul Samad Rabiu**, and **Allen Onyema** embody this evolution. Their initiatives underscore a powerful truth: when giving becomes a culture rather than an isolated act, philanthropy has the power to transform societies and shape the future of Africa.

The Economic and Social Influence of Celebrity Followers on Digital Platforms

In the digital age, celebrity followers and fans are not only passive consumers of content, but active participants in the economic and social ecosystems shaped by social media. While much attention is paid to the economic influence of celebrity endorsements, it is equally important to understand how users engage with content and how such engagement drives both social and financial outcomes.

Daily, social media feeds are flooded with breaking news, celebrity updates, viral challenges, and advice from admired figures. However, not all content is accurate or harmless. Before reacting, whether by liking, sharing, or attempting a trend, the users should pause and critically assess the content. Even a single click can propagate information to thousands, or potentially millions, amplifying both benefits and risks. Thoughtful engagement not only mitigates harm but also maximises the positive economic and social impact of digital interactions.

Celebrity-driven trends often create substantial economic incentives, from product promotions to viral marketing campaigns. Yet admiration for influencers does not guarantee accuracy or safety. Followers must cultivate skills to verify information from credible sources and recognise misleading trends. Understanding the psychological mechanisms that make content viral, such as emotional triggers, can help users navigate feeds with discernment.

Viral content, while urgent and entertaining, carries potential risks. Challenges, hacks, or "life advice" may generate short-term engagement but can result in long-term social or economic costs if harmful. Analysing case studies of viral trends highlights the importance of informed decision-making and the broader economic implications of misinformation.

Finally, the dissemination of unverified information can propagate societal and economic harm. Users who prioritise verification before sharing contribute to a healthier digital ecosystem. Highlighting instances where individuals corrected misinformation demonstrates the positive feedback loop between responsible engagement and social influence.

In summary, while celebrities shape consumer behaviour and drive economic activity online, the responsibility lies with followers to engage thoughtfully. Strategic, informed participation not only protects individual well-being but also enhances the economic and social value of digital networks.

Chapter 10

Impact of Education, Innovation, and Governance

1. Waking the Giant

In a small village on the outskirts of Nairobi, Kenya, a young girl named **Amina** stared at the dusty road leading to her school. Each morning, she walked five kilometres under the blazing sun, carrying a worn-out backpack filled with tattered notebooks. Despite the exhaustion and the odds stacked against her, she carried a dream bigger than the distance she travelled: a dream to change the world. Amina was not alone. Across Africa, countless youth face similar challenges limited resources, societal pressure, and a world that often doubts their potential.

African youth are no longer content to follow they are rising to lead, to innovate, and to redefine what it means to succeed. The transformation is not just about personal achievement. It is about shaping societies, rewriting narratives, and making Africa a continent of solutions, not problems.

The question that emerges is profound: how can ordinary African youth, like Amina, rise to global recognition and influence while remaining rooted in their communities? The answer lies at the intersection of education, innovation, and governance. These three pillars are not mere buzzwords but tools through which Africa's youth are becoming the continent's most celebrated change-makers.

2. The Power of Education

Education is often described as the great equaliser. For Africa's youth, it is the lantern that illuminates the path from uncertainty to possibility. Consider the story of Chinedu, a young man from a rural town in Nigeria. Chinedu's school lacked textbooks, computers, and even consistent electricity, yet he was driven by an insatiable curiosity. Each night, by candlelight, he devoured whatever knowledge he could find online through a borrowed smartphone.

Chinedu's hunger for learning propelled him to design a mobile app that taught coding to children in remote villages. Today, hundreds of children across Nigeria are learning to code, opening doors to global opportunities. His success was not born from privilege but from persistence, creativity, and the willingness to embrace education in all its forms.

Education is more than classrooms and exams. It is the cultivation of critical thinking, problem-solving, and a growth mindset. African youth are proving that when knowledge is paired with determination, the possibilities are limitless. Education empowers them to innovate, to challenge norms, and to step into roles of leadership that were once considered unattainable. Every young African has a story like Chinedu's waiting to unfold. The secret is simple: never underestimate the power of learning, even under challenging circumstances. Knowledge, after all, is the foundation upon which legacies are built.

3. Turning Ideas into Impact

Education lights the path, but innovation is what allows youth to walk it boldly. Across the continent, African youth are transforming ideas into solutions that tackle real-world challenges. In Kigali, Rwanda, a team of young innovators developed a drone delivery system that transports essential medical supplies to remote villages. In Lagos, Nigeria, youth-led startups are creating affordable solar energy solutions that power homes without access to the national grid.

Innovation does not require massive resources. It requires creativity, resilience, and the courage to act. It is the ability to see problems not as barriers but as invitations to create. Take the story of **Fatou**, a young Senegalese entrepreneur who turned her passion for sustainable fashion into an international brand. Using recycled materials, she created clothing that tells a story of culture, identity, and environmental responsibility. Today, Fatou's designs are showcased at fashion shows in Paris and Milan, proving that African youth can compete on the global stage while staying true to their roots.

The lesson is clear: innovation is the bridge between dreams and reality. It transforms ambition into tangible impact and demonstrates that youth are not passive recipients of opportunity. They are architects of their own futures.

4. **Leading Change Beyond Self**

While education and innovation empower the mind and spark creativity, governance instils responsibility and vision. True leadership is not about titles or fame; it is about influencing positive change and shaping the systems that govern communities. African youth are increasingly stepping into these roles, demanding transparency, accountability, and social justice.

In South Africa, youth movements have pressured governments to reform education and healthcare policies. In Ghana, young leaders are creating platforms that allow citizens to participate in decision-making processes traditionally reserved for older generations. These examples illustrate a profound truth: governance is not limited to politics; it is the commitment to serve society and uplift communities.

Leadership requires courage. It demands the ability to make difficult decisions, the wisdom to listen, and the integrity to act even when recognition is not guaranteed.

Young African leaders are showing that governance is a tool not just for personal advancement, but for collective empowerment. Imagine a continent where every village has youth councils, where innovation meets policy, and where educated, courageous youth are the standard bearers of ethical leadership. This is not a dream; it is already becoming reality.

5. **The Transformation**

The impact of African youth is now visible on the global stage. Celebrities in this context are not just entertainers but innovators, entrepreneurs, educators, and leaders who inspire millions. Their recognition comes from impact, not vanity.

Consider **William Kamkwamba** from Malawi, who built a windmill from scrap materials at age fourteen, bringing electricity to his village. His story inspired books and a Netflix adaptation. Or the Kenyan climate activist **Vanessa Nakate**, whose advocacy has influenced international climate policy. These youth are celebrated not because they sought fame, but because their actions resonated worldwide.

What sets them apart is resilience, vision, and authenticity. They pursued what mattered, remained committed to their communities, and leveraged opportunities to make a difference. Their journeys teach a powerful lesson: fame is a byproduct of meaningful action; impact is the true currency of legacy. For Africa's youth today, the path from follower to celebrity is not about imitation or shortcuts. It is about courageously embracing education, daring to innovate, and committing to leadership that transforms communities.

6. **Lessons for Every Reader**

If you are a young African reading this, understand that your journey begins now. The stories above are not exceptions but examples of what is possible when you combine vision with action. Here are the key take-aways:

1.   Pursue education relentlessly. Knowledge is power, but action makes it transformative. Learn relentlessly, even when resources are limited.

2.   Innovate boldly. See every problem as an opportunity. Small ideas can become global solutions.

3.   Lead with integrity. Leadership is service. Influence others by setting an example and making ethical choices.

4.   Stay rooted. Fame and recognition are fleeting. Impact is lasting. Let your work serve your community and your continent.

When celebrities and citizens alike treat compassion as a daily commitment rather than a camera moment, they ignite a chain reaction of empowerment. Africa doesn't need more charity; it needs champions of change who understand that giving back is not a moment of generosity but a movement of transformation.

Let every celebrity rise as a builder, a giver, and a mentor, shaping the path for the next generation to follow. As we stand at the crossroads of culture and influence, let us ask ourselves: what does it truly mean to be a celebrity in Africa today?

In the heart of our continent, where every voice matters and every life holds promise, fame must evolve. It must become more than a mirror of success; it must become a window of hope.

Our celebrities are not just entertainers. They are educators. They are healers. They are builders of dreams. They carry the power to shape minds, to shift narratives, and to spark movements. And with that power comes a sacred responsibility: to serve, to uplift, and to lead with compassion.

Let us celebrate those who use their platforms not for vanity, but for vision. Those who turn influence into impact. Those who remind us that greatness is not in how brightly you shine but in how many you help rise.

To every star rising across Africa, I say this: your legacy will not be measured by the number of followers you gain, but by the number of lives you transform, because the future of African celebrity is not in the spotlight but it is in the hearts you touch, and the communities you build, and the hope you ignite.

Chapter 11

Empowerment and Drive: Nation-Building

In Africa, celebrities are more than entertainers; they are powerful influencers capable of shaping public opinion, inspiring movements, and impacting communities. Traditionally, fame has been associated with luxury and personal success. However, in a continent rich with talent and potential, celebrity influence can be extended beyond personal gain to empower followers and contribute to nation-building. True empowerment equips individuals with knowledge, confidence, and opportunities to effect positive change in their lives and communities.

Leading by Example

African celebrities can inspire by modelling resilience, ethical behaviour, and social responsibility. Many young Africans look to public figures for guidance on navigating societal challenges such as poverty, unemployment, and inequality. Celebrities who openly share their personal journeys of overcoming adversity demonstrate that success is achievable despite obstacles. By consistently modelling integrity and responsibility, they instil values that strengthen communities and promote accountable leadership.

Promoting Education and Skill Development

Education remains one of Africa's most potent tools for empowerment. Celebrities can leverage their platforms to advocate for literacy, scholarships, vocational training, and skills development. Beyond formal education, promoting financial literacy, digital skills, and civic engagement equips followers to make informed decisions and contribute meaningfully to society. Initiatives such as mentorship programmes, workshops, or advocacy campaigns enable celebrities to create tangible opportunities for personal and professional growth.

Amplifying Social and Developmental Causes

Celebrities can bring attention to critical societal issues including healthcare, gender equality, environmental sustainability, and poverty reduction. By highlighting these challenges, they encourage followers to participate in solutions, fostering a culture of civic responsibility. For instance, supporting public health campaigns, environmental initiatives, or women's empowerment programmes transforms fame into a tool for collective impact. Through this approach, African celebrities can mobilise communities and inspire social change.

Celebrating Cultural Identity and Creativity

African celebrities can empower followers by embracing and promoting the continent's cultural heritage. Highlighting traditional music, fashion, arts, and storytelling instil pride and inspires creative self-expression. By valuing authenticity and diversity, celebrities encourage followers to explore their own talents and contribute to Africa's evolving cultural narrative. Such empowerment nurtures confidence, innovation, and a sense of belonging.

Creating Platforms for Engagement and Mentorship

The rise of social media offers celebrities unprecedented access to fans across the continent and the diaspora. Hosting online workshops, Q&A sessions, or mentorship initiatives allows celebrities to provide guidance, encouragement, and recognition. By amplifying followers' achievements and fostering interactive communities, public figures transform admiration into meaningful engagement, empowering individuals to pursue their ambitions.

Supporting Entrepreneurship and Local Economic Development

Economic empowerment is essential for sustainable development. African celebrities can support entrepreneurship by investing in small businesses, incubators, or social enterprises, as well as mentoring aspiring entrepreneurs. Promoting financial independence and economic participation enables followers to break cycles of poverty and create opportunities within their communities. By linking influence on tangible impact, celebrities demonstrate that empowerment can be both inspirational and actionable.

Advocating Mental Health and Well-Being

Mental health is a crucial dimension of empowerment that is often overlooked in Africa. Celebrities who openly discuss challenges related to anxiety, depression, or stress help reduce stigma and encourage followers to seek support. Promoting emotional resilience equips communities with the tools to navigate personal and societal challenges, fostering healthier, more confident, and proactive citizens.

African celebrities hold a unique capacity to transform fame into a force for nation-building. By leading by example, promoting education, amplifying social causes, celebrating culture, mentoring followers, supporting entrepreneurship, and advocating mental health, they empower individuals and communities alike. True celebrity influence is measured not by wealth or recognition, but by tangible contributions to society and the lives uplifted. When aligned with purpose, African celebrities can ensure that their legacy extends beyond personal success to the empowerment of their people and the sustainable development of their nations.

Chapter 12

The Future of Celebrity in Africa

What does the future hold for celebrity culture in Africa? Will fame continue to be aspirational, or will it evolve into something entirely different? As technology reshapes how we connect, create, and consume, the African celebrity landscape is undergoing a profound transformation. From AI-powered influencers to niche fame in online communities, the future of celebrity is no longer confined to red carpets and radio hits but is digital, decentralised, and deeply personal.

The Rise of Non-Human Celebrities

Imagine a celebrity who never sleeps, never ages, and never gets caught in a scandal. That's the promise of virtual influencers: AI-generated personalities who are already making waves globally and slowly entering the African digital space. These avatars, powered by algorithms and creative teams, are designed to engage audiences, promote brands, and even spark conversations.

In Africa, where storytelling and visual culture are rich and diverse, virtual influencers could become powerful tools for brands and creators. They offer a blank canvas for cultural expression, allowing designers, musicians, and marketers to craft digital personalities that reflect African aesthetics, values, and voices.

But this rise also raises questions: can a virtual being truly represent lived African experiences? Will audiences embrace non-human celebrities with the same passion as real ones? As AI becomes more accessible, the line between reality and simulation will blur and Africa will have to decide how it wants to engage with this new form of fame.

The Power of Niche Communities

Gone are the days when fame was measured by how often you appeared on national TV. Today, fame is fragmented. It lives in WhatsApp groups, Twitter threads, YouTube channels, Instagram, Facebook, and TikTok niches.

A fashion vlogger in Lagos, a tech reviewer in Nairobi, a spoken word artist in Accra—each can build loyal followings within specific online circles. These creators may not be household names, but they are influential within their communities. Their fame is intimate, authentic, and often more impactful than mainstream celebrity.

This shift empowers creators to focus on passion over popularity. It also allows for more representation regional languages, local issues, and cultural nuances, which can then flourish without needing mass appeal. Fame becomes less about being everywhere and more about being *somewhere* that matters.

For African youth, this is liberating. They no longer need to chase global stardom to feel seen. They can build meaningful careers by serving their communities, telling their stories, and staying true to their roots.

The post-Celebrity Era:

Perhaps the most radical shift is the idea that fame itself may lose its allure. In a world saturated with influencers, viral moments, and digital noise, some Africans are beginning to question the value of celebrity. Is it still aspirational or has it become exhausting?

The post-celebrity era doesn't mean people stop being famous. It means fame stops being the goal. Instead, authenticity, impact, and purpose take centre stage. Creators focus on building movements, not just followings. Audiences seek connection, not just entertainment.

In Africa, this shift is already visible. Activists, educators, and community builders are gaining recognition not for their fame, but for their work. Social media is being used to amplify causes, not just selfies. Fame becomes a byproduct of influence and not the other way around.

This evolution could redefine what it means to be a celebrity in Africa. It's no longer about being idolised but is about being *useful*. The future celebrity may be a changemaker, a storyteller, a healer, and not just a performer.

The future of celebrity in Africa is not a copy of Western trends but it's a remix, a reinvention, a revolution. It's shaped by technology but grounded in culture. It's global in reach, but local in flavour.

As the digital landscape continues to evolve, so will the people who rise within it. The next generation of African celebrities may not look like the ones we know today. They may be virtual, anonymous, or community based, but they will be powerful, relevant, and deeply connected to the continent's heartbeat.

References

1. Banky W Foundation. *bankywfoundation.org*
2. BBC News Africa. "African Celebrities as Social Influencers." *bbc.com/news/world/Africa*
3. Davido Foundation. *davidoofficial.com/foundation*
4. Guardian Nigeria. "Celebrity Influence on African Consumer Markets." *guardian.ng*
5. Guardian Nigeria. "Philanthropy and Social Responsibility Among Celebrities." *guardian.ng*
6. Omotola Jalade-Ekeinde Foundation (OYEP). *oyep.org*
7. Vanguard Nigeria. "African Celebrities Shaping Societal Values Through Giving Back." *vanguardngr.com*
8. Vanguard Nigeria. "Social Entrepreneurship Among Nigerian Celebrities." *vanguardngr.com*
9. https://vocal.media/education/poor-girl-of-nairobi
10. Today's life foundation by Mansura Isah—company, directors and contact details | nigeria24.
11. Hadiza Gabon Foundation - company, directors and contact details | Nigeria24
12. https://www.cuppyfoundation.org/
13. www.thetontodikehfoundation.org
14. https://itelemedia.com/tiwa-savage-charity-initiative-launch/
15. Punch: 'Davido announces N300m donation to orphanage homes' (20 Feb 2024). https://punchng.com/davido-announces-n300m-donation-to-orphanage-homes/
16. MyJoyOnline: 'Davido announces new donation to orphanages' (20 Feb 2024). https://www.myjoyonline.com/davido-announces-new-donation-to-orphanages/

17.   Gazette: 'Fans hail Davido for supporting 500 orphanages' (Feb 2025). https://gazettengr.com/fans-hail-davido-for-supporting-500-orphanages-across-nigeria/

18.   Akon Lighting Africa official brochure (2015). https://akonlightingafrica.com

19.   PV Magazine: 'Checking in on Akon Lighting Africa' (15 Oct 2020). https://pv-magazine-usa.com/2020/10/15/checking-in-on-akon-lighting-africa/

20.   Wikipedia: 'Akon Lighting Africa' (summary of claimed reach). https://en.wikipedia.org/wiki/Akon_Lighting_Africa

21.   Big Issue: 'All the amazing things Sadio Mané has done for charity' (profile). https://www.bigissue.com/news/activism/all-the-things-afcon-winner-sadio-mane-has-done-for-charity/

22.   Borgen Magazine: 'Senegalese Superstar Mane's Philanthropic Work' (23 Aug 2022). https://www.borgenmagazine.com/manes-philanthropic-work/

23.   Didier Drogba Foundation — official mission page. https://www.didierdrogbafoundation.org/en/our-mission

24.   Borgen Magazine: 'Drogba's charity and humanitarian work' (9 Sept 2022). https://www.borgenmagazine.com/drogbas-charity/

25.   Samuel Eto'o Foundation (profile & activities). https://www.idealist.org/en/nonprofit/c1c3a9d8b90b4373bd850caa4911e665-samuel-etoo-foundation-austin

26.   The Guardian / FIFA Foundation coverage of community programmes with Eto'o (2019). https://www.theguardian.com/football/gallery/2019/mar/19/samuel-etoo-cameroon-fifa-foundation-community-program-in-pictures

27.   Borgen Magazine: 'Mohamed Salah's Philanthropic Work in Egypt' (25 Apr 2022).

https://www.borgenmagazine.com/salahs-philanthropic-work/

28.   Middle East Monitor: 'Mohamed Salah donates to rebuild church/hospital' (17 Aug 2022). https://www.middleeastmonitor.com/20220817-mohamed-salah-donates-157000-to-rebuild-abu-sifin-coptic-church/

29.   Charlize Theron Africa Outreach Project official site & impact report (2024). https://www.charlizeafricaoutreach.org

30.   People.com coverage of CTAOP fundraising and events (2024). https://people.com/charlize-theron-support-from-twisters-stars-at-africa-outreach-project-2024-block-party-exclusive-8677940

31.   UNICEF Goodwill Ambassador page — Angélique Kidjo. https://www.unicef.org/goodwill-ambassadors/angelique-kidjo

32.   Wikipedia: Angélique Kidjo (Batonga Foundation details). https://en.wikipedia.org/wiki/Ang%C3%A9lique_Kidjo

33.   Princess of Africa Foundation (official). https://yvonnechakachaka.co.za/poaf/

34.   Save the Children South Africa: event coverage involving Yvonne Chaka Chaka. https://www.savethechildren.org.za/News-and-Events/News/South-Africa-comes-together-to-campaign-for-an-end

35.   Sheldrick Wildlife Trust: 'Lupita Nyong'o meets elephant orphans' coverage. https://www.sheldrickwildlifetrust.org/news/updates/academy-award-winning-actress-lupita-nyong-o-meets-the-elephant-orphans

36.   Glamour: 'Lupita paid for 600 kids to see Black Panther' (2018). https://www.glamour.com/story/lupita-nyongo-paid-for-600-kids-to-see-black-panther

37. Yen.com.gh: 'Wizkid projects including scholarship scheme' (profile). https://yen.com.gh/real-estate/225101-4-astounding-projects-spearheaded-by-wizkid-making-world-a-place/

38. CSR Reporters: '10 Nigerian celebrities known for their charity work' (overview). https://csrreporters.com/10-nigerian-celebrities-known-for-their-charity-work/

39. https://vdmfoundation.com/

40. https://ojyokpefoundation.com/

About the Author

Richard Owoeye, FCCA, is a distinguished professional accountant with extensive expertise in financial reporting, fintech innovation, tax management, and business development. A Fellow of the Association of Chartered Certified Accountants (ACCA) and holder of an MBA with a specialisation in finance, he has established himself as a thought leader in financial integrity, corporate ethics, and sustainable development.

Driven by a passion for leadership and humanitarian impact, Richard advocates for a new generation of African celebrities and professionals who combine excellence with empathy. His work champions the values of purpose, service, and accountability, positioning them as the true measure of influence in society.